# My Sporting Hero: World's Greatest Sporting Comebacks

## Learn about the greatest comebacks of all time

D1430735

Rob Green

# Introduction

Welcome to the exciting world of sporting comebacks! This book is all about the greatest sporting comebacks in history. A comeback is when a team or player is losing and then they come back and win the game or match. Imagine being down by a lot of points and then coming back to win against all odds, that's what a comeback is all about!

We will take you on a journey through some of the most amazing and unforgettable comebacks in the world of sports. From basketball, to football, to hockey, and even tennis, we will explore the incredible stories of athletes who refused to give up, even when it seemed like all hope was lost. You'll learn about Michael Jordan and how he led the Chicago Bulls to three NBA championships after returning from retirement. We'll also talk about Muhammad Ali, who came back to win the Heavyweight Championship after being banned from boxing for three years.

We'll also talk about the Boston Red Sox, who made one of the greatest comebacks in baseball history when they won the 2004 World Series after being down 3-0 in the American League Championship Series. You'll also hear about Martina Navratilova, who made a comeback to win the Wimbledon Ladies' Singles title after being away from the game for several years.

We'll also talk about the Liverpool FC, who made an incredible comeback against AC Milan in the 2005 Champions League final. You'll learn about Dan Marino and how he led the Miami Dolphins to the Super Bowl in 1984, after tearing his Achilles tendon the previous season. We'll also tell you about Manchester United's comeback in the 1999 Champions League final and the New York Islanders comeback to win the 1993 Stanley Cup Finals after being down 2-1 in the series.

The book is filled with exciting stories of some of the world's greatest athletes, who refused to give up and showed the world that anything is possible if you never give up. These incredible comebacks will leave you feeling inspired and motivated to never give up on your own dreams. So sit back, relax, and get ready to be amazed by some of the most incredible comebacks in sports history!

# Michael Jordan

Michael Jordan, also known as MJ, is one of the greatest basketball players of all time. He played for the Chicago Bulls for many years and helped lead them to six NBA championships. But in 1993, he decided to retire from the NBA and try his hand at baseball. He played baseball for a year or two, but eventually, he realized that his true passion was basketball. So, he decided to come back to the NBA in 1995.

He rejoined the Chicago Bulls and helped lead them to win three more championships in 1996, 1997, and 1998. It was an amazing comeback and MJ proved that he was still one of the best players in the league. Even though it was a short comeback, it was one of the most iconic moments in NBA history.

# Muhammad Ali

Muhammad Ali, also known as "The Greatest," is widely considered to be one of the greatest boxers of all time. He was the Heavyweight Champion of the World in 1964, but in 1967, he was stripped of his title and banned from boxing for three years. The reason for this was that he refused to be drafted into the United States Army to fight in the Vietnam War. He stated that he was a conscientious objector and that it was against his religious beliefs to fight in a war.

During the time he was banned from boxing, Ali continued to speak out against the war and became an influential figure in the Civil Rights Movement. He also continued to train and stay in shape, knowing that one day he would be able to fight again.

In 1970, Ali was allowed to fight again, but it wasn't until 1974 that he got his chance to fight for the Heavyweight Championship of the World once again.

His opponent was George Foreman, who was considered to be one of the most powerful and intimidating boxers of all time. Many people thought that Ali had no chance of winning, but he had a plan.

On the night of the fight, Ali used a strategy called the "rope-a-dope." He leaned against the ropes and let Foreman punch him, making Foreman tire himself out.

Then, in the eighth round, Ali unleashed a flurry of punches and knocked Foreman out. It was one of the most incredible comebacks in sports history.

Ali had regained his title as Heavyweight Champion of the World, and he had done it in a way that no one had ever seen before.

This comeback was not only a victory in the ring, but it was also a victory for Ali as a person. He had stood up for what he believed in and had been punished for it, but he had never given up. He had come back stronger than ever and had proven to the world that he was truly "The Greatest." Ali's comeback in 1974 was an iconic moment in sports history, and it cemented his legacy as one of the greatest boxers of all time.

# Boston Red Sox

The Boston Red Sox are one of the most beloved baseball teams in America, and in 2004, they made one of the greatest comebacks in sports history. They were playing in the American League Championship Series (ALCS) against the New York Yankees, and they were down 3-0 in the series. This meant that they had to win the next four games in a row in order to advance to the World Series.

At the time, no team in baseball history had ever come back from a 3-0 deficit to win a playoff series. The odds were stacked against the Red Sox, and many people thought that their season was over. But the Red Sox refused to give up. They won game four and then game five, and suddenly, they had a chance to win the series in game six.

Game six was one of the most dramatic and intense games in baseball history.

The Red Sox were down 4-3 in the ninth inning, and it looked like their comeback was going to fall short. But then, their captain, Derek Jeter, made an error, and the Red Sox scored two runs to take the lead. They won the game and forced a game seven.

In game seven, the Red Sox were down 3-0 in the fourth inning, but they refused to give up. They scored one run in the fourth, and then two more in the fifth, and then they took the lead with a home run by David Ortiz in the eighth inning. They went on to win the game and the series, and they advanced to the World Series.

In the World Series, the Red Sox faced the St. Louis Cardinals, and they swept them in four games to win their first World Series in 86 years. The comeback against the Yankees had not only been the first time in baseball history that a team had come back from a 3-0 deficit in the playoffs but also it had been the turning point for the Boston Red Sox to win the World Series.

The Boston Red Sox's comeback in the ALCS of 2004 was one of the most incredible moments in sports history. It was a comeback that defied the odds and proved that anything is possible. This moment will forever be etched in the minds of Red Sox fans and baseball fans alike, as one of the greatest comebacks of all time.

# Martina Navratilova

Martina Navratilova is one of the greatest female tennis players of all time. She dominated the sport during the 1970s and 1980s, winning 18 Grand Slam singles titles. However, in the late 1980s, Navratilova took a break from tennis to focus on other interests, such as playing professional beach volleyball and promoting her fitness business.

After several years away from the game, Navratilova made a comeback in the late 1980s and began playing tennis again. She worked hard to regain her form and fitness, and in 1990, she made it to the final of the Wimbledon Ladies' Singles tournament. Her opponent was Zina Garrison, a young player who had never won a Grand Slam tournament. Many people thought that Navratilova, at the age of 33, would have a hard time winning against a player who was in her prime.

But Navratilova proved everyone wrong. She played an incredible match, displaying all of her experience and skills. She won the match 6-4, 6-1, and she became the oldest Wimbledon Ladies' Singles champion in the Open Era. It was an incredible comeback and it was a testament to Navratilova's talent and determination.

Navratilova's comeback at Wimbledon in 1990 was not only an impressive victory on the court, but also it was a victory for her as a person.
It showed that age is just a number and that with hard work, dedication, and perseverance, anything is possible.

The comeback was also a reminder of how Martina Navratilova was one of the greatest female tennis players of all time and that her skills were not dulled despite her time away from the game.

Navratilova's comeback was an inspiration to many people, and it cemented her legacy as one of the greatest female athletes of all time. The victory at Wimbledon in 1990 was one of the most memorable moments of her career, and it will forever be remembered as one of the greatest comebacks in sports history.

# Liverpool

The 2005 UEFA Champions League Final between Liverpool and AC Milan is widely considered to be one of the greatest comebacks in sports history. The match took place on May 25th, 2005, at the Ataturk Olympic Stadium in Istanbul, Turkey.

Going into the match, AC Milan were the heavy favorites.

They had one of the best teams in Europe, with players like Andriy Shevchenko, Kaka, and Paolo Maldini. Liverpool, on the other hand, were the underdogs. They had a solid team but were not expected to win against a team as strong as AC Milan.

The match started well for AC Milan, as they scored three goals in the first half. Liverpool seemed to be out of the match, and it appeared that the game was over. But, the Liverpool manager Rafael Benitez made a tactical substitution at the half-time, bringing on Dietmar Hamann, which changed the course of the game.

In the second half, Liverpool came back with a vengeance. They scored three goals in six minutes, with a header from Steven Gerrard, and screamer from Vladimir Smicer and a penalty rebound from Alonso The match was tied 3-3, and it went into extra time. In extra time, Liverpool's goalkeeper Jerzy Dudek made a crucial save from Andriy Shevchenko's from point-blank range, which kept the game tied. The game went to penalties, and Liverpool won the shootout making them the Champions of Europe.

The comeback by Liverpool in the 2005 Champions League Final is considered to be one of the greatest comebacks in sports history, not just in football but in all sports. Liverpool had been written off by almost everyone, but they refused to give up and kept fighting until the final whistle. The match is remembered as one of the greatest moments in Liverpool's history and it has become a part of the club's legacy. The match will forever be remembered as an iconic moment in football history and a testament to the never-say-die attitude of the Liverpool players and fans.

The comeback not only showed the resilience and determination of the Liverpool team but also the belief of the club's fans. They had always believed in their team and never gave up hope, which was evident from the way they sang and supported their team throughout the match. It was a moment that united the club and its fans, and it will forever be remembered as one of the greatest moments in the history of Liverpool Football Club.

# Dan Marino

Dan Marino is considered to be one of the greatest quarterbacks in the history of the NFL. He played for the Miami Dolphins for 17 seasons and is considered one of the best players in the team's history. In 1984, Dan Marino led the Miami Dolphins to the Super Bowl, but it was not an easy journey. The previous season, he had suffered a tear in his Achilles tendon which had caused him to miss the remaining games of the regular season.

Many people thought that Marino's injury would be career-ending and that he would never be able to play at the same level again. But Marino was determined to make a comeback. He worked tirelessly to rehabilitate his injury and regain his form. He was determined to lead the Miami Dolphins back to the Super Bowl.

Marino's comeback was a success. He returned to the field in the 1984 season, and he led the Miami Dolphins to the Super Bowl.

During the regular season, he set an NFL record with 48 touchdown passes and became the first quarterback to throw for over 5,000 yards in a single season. He also led the league in passer rating and was named the NFL's Most Valuable Player.

The Miami Dolphins made it to the Super Bowl, where they faced the San Francisco 49ers. Although they lost the game, Dan Marino had a great performance throwing for 318 yards and two touchdowns. Despite the loss, Marino's comeback was a remarkable achievement and it was an inspiration to many people.

His determination and hard work had paid off, and he had proven that with the right mindset, anything is possible.

Dan Marino's comeback in 1984 was an incredible achievement and a testament to his talent, determination, and hard work. He had overcome a serious injury to lead his team to the Super Bowl and had cemented his place as one of the greatest quarterbacks in NFL history. His comeback is still remembered as one of the greatest

# Manchester United

The 1999 UEFA Champions League Final between Manchester United and Bayern Munich is widely considered to be one of the greatest comebacks in sports history. The match took place on May 26th, 1999, at the Camp Nou stadium in Barcelona, Spain.

Manchester United had been one of the best teams in Europe that season and were the favorites to win the match, but Bayern Munich had other plans.

They dominated the match from the start and scored early in the first half, leaving Manchester United trailing 1-0 at halftime. It seemed like the match was over when entering the 90th and final minute, and Bayern Munich were just second's away from winning the Champions League.

However, Manchester United refused to give up. In the 91st minute (1 minute into injury time), they scored a goal, which gave them hope. And then a minute later they scored another goal. The match ending 2-1 to United, within 2 minutes they had turned it around.

# The New York Islanders

The New York Islanders comeback to win the 1993 Stanley Cup Finals is considered one of the greatest comebacks in hockey history. The Islanders were playing against the Montreal Canadiens and were down 2-1 in the series. They were facing elimination and it seemed like their chance of winning the Stanley Cup had slipped away. But the Islanders refused to give up.

In Game 4, the Islanders won in overtime, thanks to a goal from David Volek. The series was tied 2-2, and the Islanders had new life. Game 5 was a back and forth affair, with the Canadiens taking the lead, but the Islanders managed to tie the game and take it to overtime. In Overtime, the Islanders scored the winning goal and took the lead in the series 3-2.

In Game 6, the Islanders sealed the deal, winning the game and the series 4-2. The Islanders had completed one of the greatest comebacks in hockey history, winning the Stanley Cup after being down 2-1 in the series.

It was a testament to the team's resilience, determination, and never-say-die attitude.

The comeback by the New York Islanders in the 1993 Stanley Cup Finals was a remarkable achievement and it is still remembered as one of the greatest moments in the history of the franchise. The team's ability to stay focused and come back from a deficit in the series was a testament to their character and the determination of the team and its players to win,

# Agassi

Andre Agassi is considered to be one of the greatest tennis players of all time. He won eight Grand Slam titles during his career, but his comeback win at the Australian Open in 2003 is considered one of the greatest comebacks in tennis history.

In the late 1990s, Agassi's career had hit a rough patch. He was struggling with injuries and personal issues, and his ranking had dropped as low as 141st in the world.

Many people thought that his best days were behind him, and that he would never win another Grand Slam tournament. But Agassi refused to give up.

He started working on his game and made a comeback in the early 2000s. He reached the finals of the US Open in 2000 and 2001, but he lost both times.
But in 2003, he made it to the finals of the Australian Open, and this time, he was determined to win.

His opponent in the final was Rainer Schuettler, who was a rank outsider, and many people thought that Agassi would win easily. But Agassi had to work hard for his victory, and he won the match 6-2, 6-2, 6-1.

Agassi's comeback victory at the Australian Open in 2003 was a remarkable achievement. He had come back from injury and personal struggles, and had proved that he was still one of the best players in the world.

He was the oldest player in the Open Era to win the Australian Open, and his victory was an inspiration to many people. His comeback is still remembered as one of the greatest moments in tennis history and cemented his place as one of the greatest players of all time.

# New York Giants

The New York Giants comeback to win Super Bowl XLII in 2008 is considered one of the greatest comebacks in the history of the NFL. The Giants were playing against the New England Patriots, who were heavily favored to win the game. The Patriots had one of the best teams in NFL history and were on the brink of completing an undefeated season.

The Giants were trailing 14-10 in the fourth quarter, and it seemed like the game was over. But the Giants refused to give up. They managed to score a touchdown with just 35 seconds left in the game, and the score was tied 17-17. The Patriots had one last chance to win the game, but the Giants defense made a crucial stop, and the game went into overtime.

In overtime, the Giants scored a touchdown on the first drive, and they won the game and the Super Bowl. It was a remarkable comeback and one of the biggest upsets in Super Bowl history.

The Giants had managed to beat one of the best teams in NFL history, and they had done it with a last-minute drive that will forever be remembered in the history of the NFL.

The comeback by the New York Giants in Super Bowl XLII was a remarkable achievement and a testament to the team's resilience, determination, and never-say-die attitude. It was a memorable moment for the Giants team, the fans, and the city of New York and it is still remembered as one

# The Chicago Cubs

The Chicago Cubs comeback to win the 2016 World Series is considered one of the greatest comebacks in baseball history. The Cubs were playing against the Cleveland Indians and were down 3-1 in the series. They were facing elimination and it seemed like their chance of winning the World Series had slipped away. But the Cubs refused to give up.

In Game 5, the Cubs won in extra innings and kept their hopes alive. In Game 6, the Cubs won in another extra-inning game and tied the series 3-3, forcing a Game 7. Game 7 was a back and forth affair, with the Indians taking the lead, but the Cubs managed to tie the game and take it to extra innings. In the 10th inning, the Cubs scored two runs and won the game 8-7, making them the champions of the World Series for the first time in 108 years.

The comeback by the Chicago Cubs in the 2016 World Series was a remarkable achievement and it is still remembered as one of the greatest moments in the history of the franchise. The team's ability to stay focused and come back from a deficit in the series was a testament to their character and the determination of the team and its players to win. The Cubs' victory ended the longest championship drought in the history of North American professional sports and brought joy to the city of Chicago and its fans.

# The Buffalo Bills

The Buffalo Bills comeback to win the 1992 AFC Wild Card Game is considered one of the greatest comebacks in NFL history. The Bills were playing against the Houston Oilers and were down 35-3 in the third quarter. It seemed like the game was over, and the Oilers were just minutes away from winning the game. But the Bills refused to give up.

In the third quarter, the Bills started to mount a comeback, scoring a touchdown and a field goal. They continued to score in the fourth quarter, with touchdowns from Thurman Thomas and Steve Tasker, bringing the score to 35-31. With only 16 seconds left in the game, the Bills had one last chance to win the game. They scored a touchdown, and with a two-point conversion, they tied the game 35-35.

The game went into overtime, and the Bills kicked a field goal to win the game 38-35.

The comeback by the Buffalo Bills in the 1992 AFC Wild Card Game is considered one of the greatest comebacks in NFL history. The Bills had managed to score 35 points in the second half and overtime, and they had done it with a last-minute drive that will forever be remembered in the history of the NFL.

The comeback by the Buffalo Bills was a remarkable achievement and a testament to the team's resilience, determination, and never-say-die attitude.

The game will forever be remembered as one of the most exciting and thrilling moments in the history of the NFL, and it cemented the Bills place as one of the most resilient teams in the league.

# Mario Lemieux

Mario Lemieux is considered to be one of the greatest hockey players of all time. He played for the Pittsburgh Penguins for 17 seasons and is considered one of the best players in the team's history. In the early 1990s, Lemieux was diagnosed with Hodgkin's lymphoma, a form of cancer, and he had to take a leave of absence from the NHL to undergo treatment. Many people thought that his hockey career was over, but Lemieux was determined to make a comeback.

After undergoing treatment, Lemieux returned to the ice in December 1995. He was not in top form when he came back but he was determined to regain his form and help his team win. He made a slow start but as the season progressed, he began to regain his form and by the end of the season, he had won the NHL scoring title with 161 points. He had become the first player to win the scoring title after missing a significant portion of the season due to injury or illness.

Lemieux's comeback from Hodgkin's lymphoma was an incredible achievement and a testament to his strength, determination, and hard work.

He had overcome a serious illness and had proven that he was still one of the best players in the NHL. His comeback was an inspiration to many people and it cemented his place as one of the greatest hockey players of all time.

Lemieux's comeback season will always be remembered as one of the most remarkable seasons in NHL history. He had beaten cancer and come back to lead the league in scoring, showing that he was truly one of the most remarkable and talented players in the history of the game.

# The San Francisco 49ers

The San Francisco 49ers comeback to win the Super Bowl XXIII in 1989 is considered one of the greatest comebacks in the history of the NFL. The 49ers were playing against the Cincinnati Bengals and were down 16-13 in the fourth quarter. It seemed like the game was over, and the Bengals were just minutes away from winning the Super Bowl. But the 49ers refused to give up.

With just 3 minutes and 10 seconds left in the fourth quarter, the 49ers took over on their own 8-yard line. Quarterback Joe Montana led the team on a 92-yard drive, completing 8 of 9 passes, including a touchdown pass to John Taylor with only 34 seconds left to play. The 49ers won the game 20-16 and captured their third Super Bowl victory in the decade.

The comeback by the San Francisco 49ers in Super Bowl XXIII was a remarkable achievement and a testament to the team's resilience, determination, and never-say-die attitude.

The team's ability to stay focused and come back from a deficit in the final minutes of the game was a testament to the character of the team and the determination of the players to win. It was a memorable moment for the 49ers team, the fans, and the city of San Francisco and it is still remembered as one of the greatest moments in the history of the franchise. The game was also notable for Joe Montana's performance, who was named Super Bowl MVP, and it cemented his status as one of the greatest quarterbacks in the history of the NFL.

# Brett Favre

Brett Favre is considered one of the greatest quarterbacks in the history of the NFL. He played for the Green Bay Packers, New York Jets and the Minnesota Vikings. In 2008, he retired from the NFL but after a year off, he decided to un-retire and play again. The Minnesota Vikings was looking for a quarterback and signed him for the 2009 season.

Many people thought that Favre's decision to return to the NFL at the age of 40 would be a mistake, and that he would not be able to lead the team to success. But Favre proved them wrong. He had a great season, leading the team to the NFC Championship Game, where they lost to the New Orleans Saints. Favre's performance that season was remarkable and it was a testament to his talent, determination, and hard work.

Favre's comeback season in 2009 was a remarkable achievement and it is still remembered as one of the greatest comebacks in NFL history.

He had come back from retirement and had proven that he was still one of the best players in the league. His comeback was an inspiration to many people and it cemented his place as one of the greatest quarterbacks in the history of the NFL. Despite the team's loss in the NFC Championship Game, it was a remarkable season for the Minnesota Vikings and it showed the resilience and determination of the team led by Brett Favre.

# The St. Louis Cardinals

The St. Louis Cardinals comeback to win the 2006 National League Championship Series is considered one of the greatest comebacks in baseball history. The Cardinals were playing against the heavily-favored Detroit Tigers and were down 3-1 in the series. They were facing elimination and it seemed like their chance of winning the World Series had slipped away. But the Cardinals refused to give up.

In Game 5, the Cardinals won with a dramatic home run by outfielder Scott Rolen, keeping their hopes alive. In Game 6, they won again, this time thanks to a walk-off home run by outfielder Jim Edmonds. With the series tied 3-3, the Cardinals had forced a decisive Game 7. In Game 7, the Cardinals were trailing 1-0 for most of the game, but in the 9th inning, they scored 2 runs to take the lead and win the game, thus winning the National League Championship Series.

The comeback by the St. Louis Cardinals in the 2006 National League Championship Series was a remarkable achievement and it is still remembered as one of the greatest moments in the history of the franchise. The team's ability to stay focused and come back from a deficit in the series was a testament to their character and the determination of the team and its players to win. The Cardinals went on to win the World Series that year, their 10th championship in the team's history. The comeback solidified the team's reputation of being a resilient and determined team, capable of overcoming great odds.

## Barcelona

In the 2017 Champions League Round of 16, FC Barcelona faced off against Paris Saint-Germain in one of the most dramatic comebacks in the history of the competition.

The first leg, played at the Parc des Princes in Paris on February 14th, saw PSG dominate Barcelona with a commanding 4-0 victory.. The result left Barcelona with an almost impossible task of overturning the deficit in the second leg.

The second leg, played at the Camp Nou in Barcelona on March 8th, started off with PSG looking to solidify their lead and advance to the quarterfinals.
However, Barcelona had other plans, and pulled 3 goals back, PSG replied with one of their own making it 5-3 over both legs.

Then with 2 minutes to go Barcelona scored 3 times to take them through 6-5!

This match will forever be remembered for its remarkable turnaround, as Barcelona made history with one of the most remarkable comebacks in the history of the Champions League.

# Round Up

Wow, what a journey! We've just read about some of the greatest comebacks in sports history and it's been an incredible ride. We've learned about some of the most determined and resilient athletes who refused to give up, even when it seemed like all hope was lost.

From Michael Jordan, who led the Chicago Bulls to three NBA championships after returning from retirement, to Muhammad Ali, who came back to win the Heavyweight Championship after being banned from boxing for three years, these athletes have shown us that anything is possible if you never give up.

We've also learned about some of the greatest team comebacks in sports history. The Boston Red Sox, who made one of the greatest comebacks in baseball history when they won the 2004 World Series after being down 3-0 in the American League Championship Series. The Liverpool FC, who made an incredible comeback against AC Milan in the 2005 Champions League final, and the New York Islanders comeback to win the 1993 Stanley Cup Finals after being down 2-1 in the series.

We've also learned about individual comebacks like Martina Navratilova, who made a comeback to win the Wimbledon Ladies' Singles title after being away from the game for several years, and Dan Marino, who led the Miami Dolphins to the Super Bowl in 1984, after tearing his Achilles tendon the previous season.

We hope that this book has inspired you to never give up on your own dreams, no matter how hard things may seem. These athletes have shown us that anything is possible if you believe in yourself and never give up.

As you continue to grow and pursue your own passions and interests, remember the stories and lessons of these athletes and know that with hard work and determination, you can accomplish anything you set your mind to.

Thank you for reading this book with us and we hope you have enjoyed learning about these amazing comebacks. Remember, every time you feel like giving up, just think about these athletes and their incredible stories of perseverance and determination.

They have taught us that no matter how difficult the situation may seem, with hard work and a never-give-up attitude, we can overcome any obstacle and achieve our goals.

So never give up on your dreams, no matter how hard they may seem to be. Keep pushing yourself and working towards your goals, and one day, you too may be able to make a comeback that will inspire others. Remember, anything is possible if you believe in yourself and never give up.

## What Did You Think?

First of all, thank you for purchasing this book. We know you could have picked any number of books to read, but you picked this book and for that, we are extremely grateful.

If you enjoyed this book and found some benefit in reading this, we'd love to hear from you and hope that you could take some time to post a review on Amazon. Your feedback and support will help us to know what you like.

You can do this by going to your orders on Amazon and selecting the book and then reviewing it.

Once again from the entire 'My Football Hero' family, thank you!

There are many more books to collect and we're always producing new books. Follow us on Insta @myfootballhero_ or Facebook @myfootballhero to hear about new releases.

Please don't forget to review us on Amazon, Thank you.